THE ART OF TROMBONE PRACTICE & PERFORMANCE

THE ART OF TROMBONE PRACTICE & PERFORMANCE

José Leonardo Leon, D.M.A.

Foreword by
José Valentino Ruiz, Ph.D.

DUST & ASHES
PUBLISHING COMPANY

Copyright © 2023 José Leonardo Leon, D.M.A.

All rights reserved. No part of this publication may be reproduced, distributed, or transmitted in any form or by any means, including photocopying, recording, or other electronic or mechanical methods, without the prior written permission of the publisher, except in the case of brief quotations embodied in critical reviews and certain other noncommercial uses permitted by copyright law.

For permission requests, write to the publisher, addressed "Attention: Permissions Coordinator," at the website below.

ISBN: 978-1-7360455-8-9

Library of Congress Control Number: 2023923013

First edition.

www.dapublishingco.com

To my wife and partner in this adventure called life, Maria Orozco-Leon. You are the greatest blessing I found during my undergraduate years in Miami. I love you and respect you with all my heart. Thank you for your endless patience, resilience, and support.

To my parents, Pá y Má (dad and mom), Beda José León and María R. de León, who taught me the importance of organization, humility, dedication, hard work, honesty, and love. Without your teachings and caring love I would have never become the professional, and especially, the citizen and human I am today. Pá, as a musician, thank you for teaching me through your guitar what a beautiful sound is, how to work to achieve it, and how a trombone really sounds even though that was not your musical instrument. Má, as an educator, thank you for teaching me the power of combining patience, faith, and sacrifice with learning. Those are the ultimate loving powers we need in life. Both of you taught me the power of organization combined with improvisation. In life, not everything will work as we plan, but planning will work for almost everything that comes at you. Love, compassion, faith, mind, body and soul. What a complex mechanism created by God. Both Pá and Má managed them all as if they majored in them at the university of life. There is the notion in society that parents are not perfect. However, I have learned that both of you have been the perfect parents for my siblings and I love you and will be forever thankful.

A mis Padres (Spanish)

A mis padres, Pá y Má (papá y mamá), Beda José León y María R. de León, quienes me enseñaron la importancia de la organización, la humildad, la dedicación, el trabajo duro, la honestidad y el amor. Sin sus enseñanzas y cariño nunca hubiera podido ser el profesional, pero especialmente el ciudadano y humano que soy hoy.

Pá, como músico, gracias por enseñarme qué es un sonido hermoso a través de tu guitarra, cómo trabajar para lograrlo y cómo suena realmente un trombón, aunque ese no era tu instrumento musical.

Má, como educadora, gracias por enseñarme el poder de combinar la paciencia, la fe y el sacrificio con el aprendizaje. Esos son los máximos poderes amorosos que necesitamos en la vida.

Ambos me enseñaron el poder de la organización combinado con la improvisación. En la vida, no todo funcionará como lo planeamos, pero la planificación funcionará para casi todo lo que se te presente. El amor, la compasión, la fe, la mente, el cuerpo y el alma, qué mecanismo tan complejo creado por Dios, y tanto Pá como Má, ustedes los manejaron todo como si hubiesen obtenido un título en ellos en la universidad de la vida.

Existe la noción en la vida de que los padres no son perfectos; sin embargo, he aprendido que ambos han sido los padres perfectos para mis hermanos y para mí. Los amo y estaré eternamente agradecido.

CONTENTS

Foreword by Dr. Jose Valentino Ruiz	1
Preface	3
CHAPTER 1 – Cultivating an Efficient Practice Framework	5
CHAPTER 2 – Morning Practice	11
CHAPTER 3 – Unlocking Your Inner Potential	17
CHAPTER 4 – Crafting Your Unique Sound: A Note for Educators	23
CHAPTER 5 – Organizing Your Practice with Leon's Practice Chart	29
CHAPTER 6 – Reflective Journaling for Musical Growth: Strengthening Self-Reflection and Accountability	37
CHAPTER 7 – Conquering the Stage	43
CHAPTER 8 – Engaging Stage Presence	59
CHAPTER 9 – Collaborative Practice with Other Trombonists	65
Afterword: The Journey Continues	73
Acknowledgements	77
Bibliography	79
Biographies	81

FOREWORD

It is with great pleasure and admiration that I introduce José Leonardo Leon's remarkable book, "The Art of Trombone Practice & Performance." This comprehensive guide is a testament to José's unparalleled expertise, decades of experience, and unwavering dedication to the trombone and the world of music.

What makes this book truly exceptional is its ability to resonate with musicians of all ages and skill levels. José has masterfully crafted a resource that is not only insightful and profound but also remarkably accessible. His ability to distill complex concepts into clear and practical advice ensures that readers can easily grasp and apply the wealth of knowledge contained within these pages.

José's vast experience as a performer, educator, and producer shines through in every chapter. His selflessness and genuine passion for teaching others have been evident to me as his friend and witness to his countless endeavors. He is a true arts entrepreneur and an extraordinary educator, having graced the stage with legendary musicians in orchestral, classical solo, chamber, pop, Latin jazz, and countless other genres.

"The Art of Trombone Practice & Performance" offers readers a treasure trove of valuable insights and techniques. From sound production and technique development to musical interpretation and stage presence, José covers a wide range of essential topics. His guidance on effective practice strategies, nurturing creativity, overcoming challenges, and finding joy in music is invaluable.

As I have witnessed firsthand, José's dedication to his craft extends far beyond the pages of this book. He embodies the principles he imparts, and his commitment to artistic excellence and the growth of his students is truly inspiring. Through this book, he invites you on a transformative journey, guiding you towards unlocking your true potential as a trombonist and musician.

I wholeheartedly recommend "The Art of Trombone Practice & Performance" to musicians and enthusiasts alike. Whether you are a beginner embarking on your musical journey or a seasoned professional seeking new perspectives, this book offers a wealth of wisdom and practical advice that will undoubtedly enhance your practice and performances.

May you embrace the knowledge and insights presented here, and may your passion for music shine through every note you play. I am honored to have the opportunity to introduce this remarkable work by José Leonardo Leon, a true luminary in the world of music.

Sincerely,

José Valentino Ruiz, Ph.D.
www.josevalentino.com

PREFACE

This book, "The Art of Trombone Practice & Performance," by Dr. Leon, is a comprehensive guide that explores the intricacies of trombone practice and offers valuable insights for trombone players at all levels. Dr. Leon provides a systematic approach to practice presenting a practice chart that optimizes efficiency and organization. The book emphasizes the importance of self-reflection, setting goals, and maintaining accountability through regular chart submissions. Additionally, it highlights the paramount significance of sound in trombone playing, encouraging students to cultivate a deep connection to sound and develop their unique and captivating tone. Ultimately, this book offers a transformative journey for trombone players, empowering them to unlock their full musical potential, find joy in their practice, and foster a lifelong love for the art of music.

CHAPTER 1

Cultivating an Efficient Practice Framework

In the pursuit of effective practice techniques and the development of trombone proficiency, it is essential to establish a comprehensive framework that encompasses various interconnected elements. This overarching approach aims to empower aspiring trombone players to not only improve their technical skills but also to cultivate a deep appreciation for music and enjoy the transformative experience of performing. First and foremost, the pedagogical endeavor revolves around fostering dedication and appreciation for music. It goes beyond the transmission of technical skills and focuses on nurturing a profound connection with the instrument and the art form itself. This holistic approach lays the foundation for musicians to embark on a journey of growth and self-expression.

While technical proficiency is undoubtedly crucial, it is equally important to strike a balance between technical mastery and artistic expression. The ultimate goal is to channel practice efforts towards the expressive and aesthetic dimensions of musical performance, learning how to manage the inner game of music (Green, Gallwey, et al. 1986). By instilling a sense of purpose and artistic intent, musicians can transcend technical boundaries and create deeply moving musical experiences that resonate with both themselves and their audience. Collaborative dynamics also play a significant role in effective practice techniques. Emulating the interplay between musicians in a well-coordinated ensemble encourages a comprehensive focus on the intricate details that may otherwise go unnoticed due to time constraints. By cultivating a collaborative mindset, musicians can uncover nuances, refine their interpretations, and ultimately deliver more impactful performances.

Furthermore, cultivating curiosity and embracing innovative practice strategies are paramount in enhancing the practice experience. Encouraging musicians to explore alternative approaches and unconventional exercises fosters a spirit of experimentation and continuous improvement. Embracing a culture of exploration not only keeps practice sessions engaging- it also cultivates a sense of inquisitiveness that fuels artistic growth and pushes boundaries. Acquiring refined listening skills is another crucial aspect of this practice framework. By expanding the scope of auditory exposure, musicians develop a heightened sensitivity to nuances in tone, phrasing, and musical expression. Actively engaging with diverse musical styles and studying recordings of masterful performances enhances musicians' ability to communicate and connect with their audience on a deeper level, further enriching the overall musical experience (Ruiz, et al. 2016).

In summary, the cultivation of an efficient practice framework intertwines dedication, artistic expression, collaboration, curiosity, and refined listening skills. These elements work in harmony to empower aspiring trombone players in their pursuit of mastery and the enjoyment of truly remarkable performances. By embracing this comprehensive approach, musicians can embark on a transformative journey, unlocking their full potential and honoring the essence of music itself.

Emphasizing the Primacy of Musical Expression

In this section, we explore the paramount importance of musical expression in guiding students on their musical journey. We delve into the multifaceted elements that contribute to meaningful expression, including technique, repertoire selection, and goal-setting. By honing these skills, students can bring their artistic visions to life using their instrument as a conduit for creative imagination.

A progressive mindset is cultivated through the setting of short and mid-term goals allowing students to approach their long-term aspirations incrementally. This approach fosters continuous growth and appreciation for the process, and guards against complacency or frustration. Building confidence in one's abilities, recognizing the gradual nature of growth, and establishing a well-structured practice routine are crucial steps in the journey toward self-assurance. Students learn to value patience, perseverance, and the transformative process of continuous improvement. By allocating practice time strategically and incorporating practice mutes, students create an environment conducive to focused and immersive practice experiences. Through this comprehensive approach, students develop their confidence, unlock their artistic potential, and embody the primacy of musical expression.

In the pursuit of guiding students toward meaningful musical expression, a comprehensive approach is essential. This approach encompasses various elements such as technique, repertoire selection, and goal-setting, which serve as indispensable tools to unlock the creative essence of musical imagination. By honing these skills, students can bring to life the sounds they envision, channeling their artistic vision through the resonating bell of their instrument.

A crucial aspect of this process involves nurturing a progressive mindset where short and mid-term goals are viewed as instrumental resources. By setting these goals, students can approach their ultimate aspiration, the long-term goal, in a step-by-step manner. This approach guards against frustration when facing unrealized objectives and prevents complacency upon their achievement. It fosters a sense of continuous growth and encourages students to appreciate the journey as much as the destination.

To cultivate a genuine appreciation for the art of music-making and foster an unwavering commitment to its pursuit, students must first acquire confidence in their own capabilities. This journey towards self-assurance unfolds through a sequence of steps designed to build a strong foundation.

The initial step involves establishing belief in one's abilities. This stage requires dedicated instruction and practice as individuals gradually develop a growing sense of self-confidence. Through consistent effort and tangible improvements, students gain the assurance needed to face musical challenges and explore their potential.

Recognizing the gradual nature of growth is another vital aspect. Patience becomes a valuable virtue as students understand that significant advancements occur over time. They come to appreciate that musical development is a journey requiring perseverance and dedication. By embracing this mindset, students shift their focus from seeking rapid results to valuing the transformative process of continuous improvement.

Distinguishing between practice routine and practice structure is also critical. Establishing a well-organized practice structure helps students overcome common pitfalls that hinder their commitment. It involves allocating practice time based on specific goals and objectives. College students, for example, may be advised to engage in sessions lasting 35 to 45 minutes, while high school students can allocate 15 to 25 minutes depending on their schedule and available resources. This thoughtful allocation of time ensures that practice sessions are purposeful and efficient.

Moreover, time allocation and strategic sessions play a significant role in optimizing practice routines. Morning sessions are recommended as the first practice session, ideally initiated as early as possible. An afternoon session follows, and the day concludes with an early or late evening session, taking into account space availability and resource access. Additionally, utilizing practice mutes, such as attaching a pillow to a chair, can create a conducive environment that promotes focused and immersive practice experiences.

By diligently following this process and embracing a structured practice routine, aspiring musicians can enhance their confidence, achieve incremental growth, and unlock the boundless joy inherent in the act of making music. This holistic approach empowers students to express themselves artistically, fulfilling their potential as musicians and deepening their connection to the transformative power of music. It is through this dedicated and thoughtful journey that students truly embody the primacy of musical expression.

CHAPTER 2

Morning Practice

Session 1: Unleashing Musicality through Airstream Manipulation

Just like breakfast is the most important meal of the day, morning sessions are the most important of all practice sessions. For this reason, this chapter will be devoted to this particular session. In this morning's practice session, we delve deeply into the foundational aspects of breath control and articulation, unlocking the boundless potential for musicality through deliberate manipulation of our airstream. The primary objective of this chapter is to cultivate a profound understanding of how our breath influences the music we create and to instill in students a sense of curiosity and exploration that propels their musical growth.

Central to this session is the prominence of decisive air management as we embark on a transformative journey to explore the vast possibilities of our breath. Recognizing the pivotal role of intentional breath control, we delve into the fundamental question: "What can we achieve with our air?" By refining our ability to discern musicality solely through the shaping and mastery of our airstream, we establish a profound connection between the visualization of sound and its translation onto our instruments.

This session emphasizes the indispensable link between assimilating the sound concept and effectively translating it into our instrumental performances. Understanding this connection from the early stages of musical development lays a solid foundation for fostering unwavering dedication to the craft. To support this process, resources such as Arnold Jacobs' philosophy on singing can be explored, offering valuable insights into the development of a well-defined sound concept (Frederiksen et al. 1996).

Recommended tools for this practice session encompass a spirometer, small breathing aids, and a mouthpiece extension tube. These tools facilitate a comprehensive exploration of breath control and its profound impact on sound production, enabling us to delve into the nuanced intricacies of their playing.

To infuse an element of playfulness into the practice routine, I propose integrating a diverse array of fundamental exercises within an engaging game-like structure. This approach combines components such as lip slurs, scales, long tones, valve exercises, and range expansion, presenting them as cohesive and organized challenges. By strategically rotating technique methods such as those written by Allen Ostrander, Arnold Jacobs, and Michel Becquet, alongside scale variations on a daily basis, we can maintain an organized and stimulating practice regimen, deriving both structure and enjoyment from their practice sessions.

Through this focused morning practice session, we can develop superior breath control, articulate with precision, and nurture a sense of curiosity and exploration. By honing these essential skills, they not only unlock the immense potential for musical expression but also lay a formidable foundation for their ongoing musical journey.

Session 2: Exploring Melodious Studies, Etudes, and Technical Books

In this session, our focus shifts to delving into melodious studies, etudes, and technical books to enhance our musical proficiency. By incorporating key elements such as scales, sight-singing, articulation, and conducting, we can further develop our musicality and expressiveness.

To begin, it is crucial to prepare ourselves before diving into an etude. One important step is to ascertain the key of the etude and practice the corresponding scale. Challenging ourselves further, we can explore the relative minor version of the scale. Utilizing tools like a drone and metronome can help us establish a solid foundation by setting the drone to the tonic of the phrase.

When selecting a Bordogni etude, for example, we should focus on a short phrase and approach it with the intention of making it musical. Taking the time to sing the etude in the manner we envision playing it allows us to internalize the musicality and bring it to life on our instrument.

Incorporating singing as an integral part of the practice process is a valuable technique. By developing the ability to conduct ourselves, visually conceptualize rhythms, and identify their corresponding beats, we enhance our overall musical understanding. Singing through etudes helps us connect with the music on a deeper level and improves our interpretive skills.

Articulation plays a crucial role in expressing the shape and character of notes. Drawing insights from renowned musicians such as Norman Bolter and Tim Higgins, we can learn how to use articulation to emulate words and enhance our musical communication. It is through mastering articulation vocabulary that we can bring clarity and nuance to our playing.

The connection between our breath and the slide is essential. By employing the concept of air-singing, we can use our slide to navigate melodic phrases. Developing slide recognition skills and connecting them seamlessly with the flow of our breath allows us to create a cohesive and expressive musical line.

As an experiment, we can explore tongueless playing, relying solely on the connection between the air and sound production. This technique aims to create a continuous sound experience, akin to playing a long, sustained note while traversing through smaller pitches in a melodic phrase. By mastering this approach, we can achieve a greater sense of legato and fluidity in our playing.

Understanding the nature of air and its transformation into waves can deepen our understanding of sound production. Visualizing this process, similar to water turning into snow, helps us grasp the physical properties involved in creating and shaping sound.

Mentally evoking the concept of Professor Dr. William Stanley from CU Boulder, "TONGUEANDAIR," which represents the coordinated action between the tongue and the air during articulation, can aid in achieving a more controlled and precise sound. This concept reminds us of the importance of balancing these elements in our playing.

Referencing Maestro Charlie Vernon's insight on "The Death of TWA," we understand the significance of producing a direct sound without excessive tongue interference. This concept encourages us to refine our technique to create a focused and powerful sound.

Incorporating these elements into our practice routine will cultivate a heightened sense of musicality, technical proficiency, and expressive communication through our instrument. By exploring melodious studies, etudes, and technical books with intention and dedication, we can continue to grow as musicians and tap into the enjoyment and fulfillment that music brings.

CHAPTER 3

Unlocking Your Inner Potential

In this section, we delve into the realm of trombone performance and explore the path to experiencing the true enjoyment of music. Building upon the foundations established in the previous section, our focus now shifts to the practical application of acquired skills and the transformative power of music. With a deep belief in our abilities as musicians and a commitment to nurturing our inner potential, we embark on a journey that will enable us to deliver engaging and confident performances. Through techniques such as focused attention, minimizing self-interference, dedicated practice, and the mastery of scales and fundamentals, we aim to unlock the joy of musical expression and tap into the profound connection between performer and audience. Let us embark on this enriching exploration, as we strive to achieve the highest level of satisfaction and fulfillment through our trombone playing.

To begin, it is crucial to acknowledge our potential as musicians. Every individual has the ability to be the best performer they can be and to deliver outstanding music performances. Believing in our abilities and trusting that we have developed the necessary skills through our diligent practice lays the foundation for a confident and engaging performance.

In their book "The Inner Game of Music," Timothy Gallwey and Barry Green introduce the concept of Self 1 and Self 2. Self 1 represents the analytical and learning side of our brain, which has acquired the necessary skills. Self 2 represents our inner creative side. During performances, it is important to transfer the information from Self 1 to Self 2 and allow our creative side to take over. This shift in focus enables us to immerse ourselves in the music and let our potential shine (Green, Gallwey, et al. 1986).

Choosing a specific focus of attention during performances is a powerful technique. By selecting one aspect of our playing, such as the airstream flowing through the trombone, we can direct our attention and fully engage with the music. This focused attention allows us to enjoy the musical experience and let our expressive abilities flourish.

Avoiding self-interference is crucial for delivering a successful performance. Self-interference refers to the self-sabotaging thoughts or actions that hinder our performance. By developing a strong focus of attention, we can minimize self-interference and allow our skills to flow naturally and effortlessly.

Practicing the entire repertoire from start to finish without interruption is an effective exercise in preparing for performances. This dedicated practice helps us develop the ability to perform the entire piece confidently and builds the necessary stamina. By repeating this process diligently and patiently, we can strive for fewer mistakes and a more polished performance each time.

When practicing small passages within the repertoire, repetition is key. Playing these passages repeatedly, around 10 to 12 times in a row, reinforces muscle memory and helps us become more comfortable with those specific sections. This focused repetition allows us to overcome challenges and perform with greater precision.

True enjoyment of our own performance is achieved when we have developed a strong commitment to music and a well-structured practice routine. During a performance, a powerful moment of realization may occur where we feel a sense of detachment observing ourselves and the entire section from above the stage. This experience signifies that we have achieved a great performance and a deep connection with the music.

Mastering scales in all possible combinations and keys is essential. Scales are not only the heart of music, but also the key to practicing our fundamentals and acquiring a strong foundation of skills. Familiarity with scales enables us to focus on the new skills we are learning rather than being hindered by unfamiliar keys.

Emphasizing fundamentals is crucial as they provide the key to success in achieving a commitment to music. Advanced skills are built upon a deep understanding of the fundamentals. By continually refining and emphasizing our fundamental techniques, such as breath control, embouchure, and articulation, we establish a solid foundation that supports our musical expression and performance.

By integrating these strategies into our practice routine and performances, we can achieve the enjoyment of music and tap into our inner potential as trombone players. The combination of a strong practice structure, technical proficiency, and expressive communication allows us to deliver captivating performances and experience the transformative power of music.

It's important to note that simply practicing pieces from start to finish repeatedly, without addressing and fixing mistakes, will only reinforce those mistakes. To avoid this, follow the steps outlined in sessions 2 and 3 for effective learning. Incorporate buzzing, which involves singing with your lips as if they were vocal chords, as a helpful tool in fixing passages; but remember not to make it the sole focus of your practice. When buzzing, ensure that you only buzz the specific music you will be playing to maintain focus and efficiency. Avoid buzzing random sounds, as it becomes ineffective in that case. By following these guidelines, you can maximize the effectiveness of your practice and improve your overall performance.

Performance Mastery

To enhance trombone performance, a strong focus on fundamental practice and repertoire integration is essential. Incorporating key tools and techniques, including tonal energy, spirometers, small tubes, and alternative mutes, establishes a solid foundation for sound production, breath control, and efficient airflow. This enables a seamless integration of scales, fundamentals, and musical elements into the repertoire.

The incorporation of fundamental practices immediately improves our playing. Connecting these fundamental concepts directly to the repertoire allows us to witness tangible advancements and reinforces the importance of regular practice. This fosters the development of practice structure skills as we recognize the direct impact of fundamentals on our overall performance.

Integrating scales into specific pieces enhances our understanding of key relationships and improves our technical proficiency. By reading music slowly and attentively, we can focus on the intricate details and nuances of the music, forging a deeper connection and enabling a more refined interpretation.

> In a group setting, it is crucial to help students adapt their individual practice routines to the classroom environment. Aligning individual and collective goals creates a productive and harmonious learning atmosphere, fostering teamwork and ensemble playing skills. This collaborative approach allows students to take responsibility for the group's progress while honing their individual abilities.

Vocalization exercises play a vital role in promoting self-awareness and enhancing overall performance. Singing cultivates a strong sense of melody, phrasing, and musicality, enabling us to internalize the music and communicate our artistic vision through our instruments.

In conclusion, the integration of fundamental practice, repertoire, and vocalization is paramount for strengthening trombone performance. This approach brings immediate improvement, develops practice structure skills, effectively applies scales to repertoire, enhances attention to detail, encourages adaptation to the classroom setting, and fosters self-awareness. Through these combined elements, we can develop a genuine commitment to and enjoyment of music while playing the trombone.

CHAPTER 4

Crafting Your Unique Sound
A Note for Educators

As educators, it's crucial never to lose sight of the true purpose behind learning and teaching the techniques of our respective instruments. It's all too easy for even the most organized students to approach their practice sessions with a mechanical checklist of technical exercises devoid of any genuine connection to the music. The unfortunate outcome of this approach is that they become mere robots, proficient at playing clean notes, pitches, and rhythms, but lacking any true joy or musicality. On the other hand, unorganized students face an even greater struggle as they may not even achieve the modest gains of their organized counterparts, burdened by frustration and mental fatigue. The solution lies within a simple approach:

Igniting Curiosity. Our students need to grasp what constitutes a good sound. Frequently, they are unaware of what defines excellence in this realm. Moreover, they must learn to discern and appreciate the nuances of different sounds within various genres. What might be considered a good sound in a commercial context may differ from what is valued in an orchestral setting, and vice versa. Even within the same genre, what constitutes a pleasing solo sound for a recital may not align with what is considered exceptional for performing a Mahler Symphony or a Mozart Opera.

Personal Story

Allow me to share a personal example from my own musical journey. The trombone was not my initial instrument of choice. In fact, it didn't even register on my radar. My perception of the trombone was tainted by the less-than-ideal examples of its sound that I had encountered. However, my father, an incredible commercial multi-string player with expertise in bass, guitar, mandolin, Cuban tres, Venezuelan cuatro, and more, possessed a discerning ear for beautiful sound. When El Sistema arrived in my town, I found myself with a choice between percussion or trombone, though my heart yearned to play the flute or cello rather than the trombone. Upon returning home, disheartened and empty-handed, my father inquired about my instrument selection. I deliberately omitted mentioning the trombone, but he sensed my dissatisfaction. My father then visited the school of music, approaching the teacher in charge who happened to be one of his former students, to ascertain the situation. When he returned, he asked me directly, "Were you offered a trombone?" I muttered an affirmative response. Prompted by curiosity, my father proceeded to play some tape recordings he had made during several nights of capturing brass music from the national radio station. It was then that I discovered the likes of the Empire Brass, the Canadian Brass, the German Brass, and the Simon Bolivar Symphony Brass (who would later become some of my teachers). I had been exposed to the magnificent sound of brass and the trombone. Those sounds became ingrained in my mind's eye. I yearned to emulate them. They became the driving purpose behind my scales, lip slurs, slide technique, mouthpiece buzzing, breathing exercises, and various other aspects of brass playing. As educators, we must follow in my father's footsteps.

My father served as my first guide in unraveling the mystery of a good sound. He kindled curiosity and purpose within my practice. Often, students have yet to encounter exceptional sound and this lack of exposure can be the root cause of their struggle to find purpose within the practice room, ultimately leading them to give up on practicing altogether.

Guide students along the path to discovering what constitutes a remarkable sound. Ignite their curiosity by encouraging them to emulate exemplary sources and visualize themselves producing that sound. In the past, my father relied on tapes while some teachers utilized video recordings and live concerts. Nowadays, the resources available are endless: YouTube, Google, the internet at large. Encourage students to ask questions, to listen to a wide array of music spanning trombone, cello, singers, classical, commercial, jazz, and world genres. Encourage them to absorb the art of singing from various artists, from the operatic prowess of Placido Domingo to the melodious jazz stylings of Frank Sinatra. For those aspiring to the bass trombone, inspire them with the deep tones of Barry White. Foster creativity through the vocalizations of Ella Fitzgerald and explore the high range by studying the performances of Mariah Carey or Rene Fleming.

Unveiling the Distinction Between Motivation and Willpower

One of the most formidable challenges in teaching trombone students lies in guiding them to set meaningful goals. At this juncture, we must ensure that they comprehend the fundamental difference between motivation and willpower. Often, students base their short and midterm goals solely on motivation. Examples may include auditioning for All-State or Solo and Ensemble competitions, preparing for recitals, securing ensemble placements, pursuing graduate studies, or aspiring to join professional ensembles during college. These goals are specific and closely tied to the concept of motivation. Consequently, once these goals are achieved (regardless of the outcome) students may lose interest and fail to perceive the necessity of sustained dedication to their practice.

On the other hand, when the broader goal—such as becoming an exceptional trombone player, collaborating with remarkable musicians, or attaining a performance level that reflects their commitment to music—replaces the specifics, it is willpower that emerges as the steadfast source of motivation. It empowers students to dedicate themselves continuously to their craft, pursuing the sheer joy of making music, while using short and midterm goals as stepping stones towards the ultimate goal: a lifelong commitment to and enjoyment of music. In this context, I often impart the insightful words of Douglas Yeo, the former bass trombonist of the Boston Symphony Orchestra:

"If you practice, you get better.
If you get better, you play with better players.
If you play with better players, you play better music.
If you play better music, you have more fun.
If you have fun, you want to practice more.
If you practice more, you get better…"

The underlying thread connecting all accomplished musicians is their unwavering commitment and profound enjoyment of music.

When devising a plan, emphasize the act of making music itself. Technique, materials, and short/midterm goals are merely resources that channel the music flowing from your imagination through your instrument, resonating from your bell. Teach trombone students to regard short and midterm goals as invaluable tools on their journey toward the ultimate goal—progressing steadily toward a long-term vision. By avoiding the pitfall of treating these shorter goals as "ultimate goals" themselves, we mitigate the risk of students experiencing frustration if they fall short or complacency if they achieve them. Focusing on the overarching objective of committing to and finding joy in music ensures that students develop the willpower necessary not only to thrive in their musical endeavors but also to cultivate their artistry, expressiveness, and overall way of life over an extended period.

CHAPTER 5

Organizing Your Practice with Leon's Practice Chart

Let me present you with a glimpse of the chart I've meticulously constructed for my college students. This chart closely resembles the one I personally utilize (the professional version) and the one I employ with my outreach studio students. It follows a two-part structure designed to optimize practice efficiency.

First and foremost, each practice session should adhere to a time limit of 45 to 50 minutes. This duration allows for essential decompression and recovery, both physically and mentally. Breaking down the material into manageable sections is key. Instead of attempting to play the entire piece from start to finish each day, it is more effective to add new sections incrementally. This approach ensures thorough learning and prevents overwhelming oneself with excessive information. Just like solving a math problem, where each formula is mastered individually before combining them into a comprehensive solution.

Leon's Practice Chart
Organizing Your Daily Goals for the 3 E's:
Efficiency, Enjoyment, and Enlightening Practice Time

Daily Practice Log. Date:_____
Trombone Studio | Dr. Leon

PART I – The Practice – Enjoy the Process

No. of Sessions _____

Session(s) Time(s): S1_____   S2_____   S3_____

Session 1

Warm Up	Lip Slurs	Scales

Break___

Session 2 (Apply Fundamentals to Music)

Method Book (s) Lyrical	Method Book (s) Technical	Solo Piece

Break____

Session 3 (Practice for the Job)

Ensemble (s) Repertoire	Excerpts or Audition Rep.	Practice for the Job	Warm-Down

Break____

PART II – The Results, The Self-Reflection

1. Goal of the Day | Improvement Today: Yes___ No___

   Yes, what went well? /**No**

   Reason_____

2. Will I change anything tomorrow? Yes___ No___

   Reason/Purpose: _____

3. Goal per Session Achieved (Circle Yes or No):

   Session 1: Yes   No   Session 2: Yes   No   Session 3: Yes   No

   If you circle **YES**, congratulate yourself, go for a treat, reward yourself…

If you circle **NO**, it's reflection time:

What do I need to change to make my goals attainable?

_____
_____
_____
_____

4. Grade your performance today on a scale of 1-10, with 10 being the highest: _____

Now, let's delve into the first part of the chart, which focuses on organizing the practice process.

Part I

Let's explore the first part of the chart, where we outline the recommended practice sessions and their respective objectives. Please note that the specific timings can be adjusted according to the student's schedule and preferences.

Session 1: This session is ideally conducted in the earlier morning hours, before 9:30 or 10:00 AM. During this time, our bodies are fresher making it perfect for warm-ups and fundamental exercises. Focus on activities such as scales, lip slurs, long tones, and other fundamental techniques. This section serves as the foundation for the day, helping you acquire new skills and address any technical deficiencies you may have noticed. After completing session one, take a short break of around 15 minutes. If there are no immediate activities, use this time for relaxation or transition to your next scheduled task.

Session 2: It's time to apply the foundation you revised or learned in session 1 to your musical abilities. The ideal timing for this session is late morning or early afternoon, after lunch. Here, you should practice both lyrical and technical methods. If you have solo repertoire, include it in this session, especially if it's a single piece. However, if you are preparing for a solo recital with multiple pieces, you may need to allocate part of the next session or a full session solely for that repertoire. Take a slightly longer break after this session considering the larger workload compared to Session 1.

Sessions 3 and/or 4: These sessions are dedicated to practicing for your specific musical commitments. If you are working towards a solo recital, these sessions should be devoted to your repertoire. If you don't have a solo recital coming up, focus on what I call "practicing for the job." College students should include ensemble repertoire (wind ensemble, jazz band, orchestra, chamber groups), orchestral excerpts, audition repertoire, and any other music related to actual gigs or jobs outside of the college realm. For high school or middle school students, this is the time to practice for school ensembles and other goals like Solo and Ensemble competitions, All-State or All-County auditions, or Youth Orchestra programs. Schedule these sessions in the early to late afternoon hours, considering household and neighbor sensitivities to sound.

Just as important as the warm-up section in Session 1 is the warm-down section in the last session. The warm-down is designed to help your body and mind relax and prepare for the next day. Perform exercises similar to the warm-up routine but in reverse. Start with more active and louder playing, gradually transitioning to soft and slower playing. Playing the trombone requires establishing a daily connection with the instrument, akin to the movie "50 First Dates" with Drew Barrymore and Adam Sandler. Just as Sandler had to make Barrymore fall in love with him every single day due to her illness, the trombone requires the musician to cultivate a loving relationship with it. As the student diligently follows this chart, great habits are developed, and the trombone becomes more responsive and enjoyable. The warm-up and warm-down sessions become shorter, taking only a matter of minutes instead of hours (Clear et al. 2018).

CHAPTER 6

Reflective Journaling for Musical Growth: Strengthening Self-Reflection and Accountability

In the pursuit of musical excellence, the ability to self-reflect holds immense significance. It is within this chapter that we explore the profound impact of self-reflection and accountability on this musical journey.

To truly understand the purpose behind our practice, we must develop the skill of evaluating progress objectively. This entails identifying areas of improvement and acknowledging where we may fall short. A valuable tool in this process is the practice chart, which provides automatic feedback to guide us in assessing our readiness for upcoming lessons or performances. Through regular self-reflection, we gain a clear sense of how far we are from achieving our ultimate goal: discovering our unique and beautiful sound, wholeheartedly committing to the art of music, and deriving joy from our performances and musical experiences.

Within the self-reflection section, we are encouraged to set two types of goals. The first type is the "goal of the day," which encompasses the cumulative progress we strive to achieve across all our practice sessions. This overarching goal directs our attention to our overall development and growth as musicians. Additionally, we are prompted to establish individual and specific goals for each practice session. For instance, during session 2, we might aim to apply a steady rhythm to the technical exercises found in the Selected Studies book by Voxman, focusing specifically on Lesson 10 and mastering the first eight measures. By consistently accomplishing these smaller goals throughout our practice sessions, we gradually fulfill our overall goals for each session and, ultimately, for the entire day.

In the pursuit of musical growth, it is equally essential for us to acknowledge and celebrate our achievements and progress. Setting a designated time for reward after a successful session allows us to appreciate our small triumphs along the way, reinforcing our motivation and cultivating a positive mindset towards our practice.

FOR THE EDUCATOR

To ensure accountability and maintain progress tracking, an expectation is set for students to submit a minimum of 5 or 6 charts per week. This is equivalent to completing one chart per day between their lessons. Such a practice fosters consistency and active engagement with their practice routine. The number of logs students bring and the content within the self-reflection section provide valuable insights into their lessons and the trajectory they are following towards success. Through diligent maintenance of these logs and thoughtful reflection on their practice experiences, students demonstrate unwavering dedication, effort, and commitment to their musical progress.

The power of self-reflection and accountability cannot be overstated in the pursuit of musical growth. By embracing self-reflection, we gain a deeper understanding of our progress, set meaningful goals, and celebrate our achievements. When coupled with accountability, we become empowered to actively engage with our practice routine, paving the way for consistent progress and a fulfilling musical experience.

In order to harness the power of self-reflection and accountability in your musical growth, Dr. José Ruiz and I have designed an assignment that will guide you towards a deeper understanding of your practice sessions and overall progress. This assignment, known as Reflective Journaling for Musical Growth, will provide you with a dedicated space to reflect on your practice experiences, identify areas of improvement, celebrate your achievements, and set goals for future sessions. By engaging in regular journaling, you will enhance your self-awareness, cultivate a positive mindset, and establish a strong sense of accountability towards your musical development. Through this assignment, you will embark on a transformative journey of self-discovery and continuous improvement in your musical journey (Ruiz, et al. 2016).

Assignment: Reflective Journaling for Musical Growth

Objective: To strengthen the power of self-reflection and accountability in your musical growth by engaging in regular journaling.

Instructions

1. Obtain a dedicated journal or notebook that will serve as your reflective journal throughout this assignment.
2. Set aside a specific time each day for journaling. This could be after your practice sessions or at the end of the day.
3. Begin each journal entry by reflecting on your practice session or musical experiences of the day. Consider the following prompts:
    a. What were your goals for the session, and did you accomplish them?
    b. What specific challenges did you face during your practice, and how did you overcome them?
    c. What areas of your playing did you notice improvement in?
    d. Were there any areas where you felt you fell short or struggled?
    e. How did you feel emotionally during your practice and after?
4. Write about any insights or observations you gained from your practice session. Consider the following questions:
    a. Did you discover any new approaches or techniques that worked well for you?
    b. Were there any moments of breakthrough or aha moments?
    c. What did you learn about yourself as a musician through this practice session?

5. Take a moment to celebrate your achievements and successes. Write about any small triumphs or progress you made, no matter how small or insignificant they may seem.
6. Reflect on the overall trajectory of your musical growth. Consider your long-term goals and how each practice session contributes to your progress. Write about any adjustments or modifications you might need to make in your practice routine or approach.
7. Finally, conclude each journal entry with a commitment to your musical growth. Set specific goals for your next practice session or highlight areas you want to focus on. Emphasize the importance of accountability in your journey.
8. Repeat this reflective journaling process daily or as frequently as possible, maintaining consistency throughout the week.
9. At the end of each week, take some time to review your journal entries. Look for patterns, recurring themes, and areas of growth. Use this reflection as a basis for adjusting your practice routine and setting new goals for the upcoming week.

Remember, this reflective journaling assignment is not only a means of documenting your progress but also an opportunity for deep self-reflection and growth. By actively engaging in this practice, you will strengthen your self-awareness, develop a stronger sense of accountability, and cultivate a mindset focused on continuous improvement in your musical journey.

CHAPTER 7

Conquering the Stage

In the captivating world of trombone performance, the stage transforms into both a canvas and a battleground, where musicians strive to express themselves fully and captivate their audiences. But the pressures and anxieties that accompany performing can sometimes overshadow our ability to shine. Fear not, for within these pages, we shall embark on a transformative journey of performance preparation, offering invaluable insights and techniques to help you navigate performance anxiety and deliver compelling performances. (Rotella, et al. 1995)

As we delve into this chapter, we shall uncover the essential components of performance preparation, equipping you with the tools needed to conquer the stage with confidence and poise. Through a harmonious blend of mental fortitude and stage presence, you will discover the secrets to unlocking your true potential as a performer.

Firstly, we shall address the intricacies of mental and emotional preparation. Here, we shall dive deep into the labyrinth of performance anxiety, unraveling its enigmatic nature and discovering how it affects us both physically and mentally. Armed with this understanding, we shall explore proven strategies to cultivate mental resilience and embrace a positive mindset. Visualization techniques shall become your trusted allies, empowering you to envision success and channel your inner strength. Moreover, we shall uncover the power of breath and relaxation, enabling you to find serenity amidst the storm of anticipation. Through mindful rehearsal and positive affirmations, you will foster unwavering self-belief and banish self-doubt, stepping onto the stage with unwavering confidence.

But performance mastery extends beyond the realm of the mind. It demands a commanding stage presence that captivates audiences and breathes life into your music. In this chapter, we shall explore the art of effective stage presence, empowering you to connect deeply with your audience and leave an indelible mark on their hearts. From commanding body language to purposeful gestures, we shall delve into the nuances of physical expression, ensuring that your presence on stage becomes a captivating performance in itself. We shall also navigate the terrain of recovery, teaching you how to gracefully navigate unexpected mishaps and transform them into moments of artistic brilliance.

Dear reader, the stage beckons you with its alluring embrace. It is time to shed the shackles of anxiety and embrace the transformative journey that awaits you. Allow the wisdom contained within this chapter to be your guiding light as you master the art of performance. With an unwavering passion for your craft and a commitment to honing your skills, you shall command the stage with confidence and captivate audiences with your magnetic presence. Embrace the power within you, and let your music transcend the boundaries of the stage, resonating deeply in the hearts and souls of all who bear witness to your artistry. The stage is your sanctuary, and with each performance, you shall leave an indelible mark upon the world.

Understanding Performance Anxiety

In the realm of music, the stage transforms into a battleground where self-expression thrives. Within this arena, we encounter a formidable foe known as performance anxiety. It is a companion that accompanies many musicians on their journey, casting a veil of doubt and unease over their performances. Our quest in this section is to unravel the enigmatic nature of performance anxiety peering beneath its surface to gain a deeper understanding of its essence.

Performance anxiety emerges from the high stakes and expectations tied to public performances. As musicians, we pour our hearts and souls into our craft, and when the moment arrives to share our music with the world the weight of anticipation can manifest as anxiety. Physiologically, performance anxiety triggers a cascade of responses within our bodies. Our heart rates quicken, our breathing becomes shallow, and our muscles tense as if preparing for a battle. Simultaneously, it infiltrates our minds sowing seeds of self-doubt and clouding our focus with negative thoughts.

However, performance anxiety is not solely a physical phenomenon. It intricately weaves itself into the fabric of our psyche affecting our thoughts, emotions, and overall mental well-being. The fear of judgment, the pressure to meet expectations, and the apprehension of making mistakes can consume us eroding our confidence and undermining our ability to perform at our best.

By delving deeper into the nature of performance anxiety, we can demystify its hold on us. Understanding that it is a natural response to the circumstances we face as musicians allows us to adopt a proactive mindset. Acknowledging that even the most seasoned performers experience anxiety offers solace and reassurance that we are not alone in our struggles.

As we embark on this exploration of performance anxiety, remember that understanding is the first step towards liberation. Illuminating its physiological, psychological, and emotional components equips us with the tools to navigate its labyrinthine pathways. With each chapter that unfolds, we shall delve further into the realm of performance anxiety, unraveling its secrets and discovering strategies to conquer its grip. The stage eagerly awaits your triumphant arrival, and armed with knowledge as your ally, you shall emerge as the master of your own performance destiny.

Unmasking the Impacts on Your Performance

The weight of performance anxiety can cast a shadow over your playing, influencing not only your technical execution, but also your overall performance. As we explore this topic further, it becomes evident that performance anxiety encompasses a range of effects that can manifest both physically and mentally. Understanding these effects is paramount to conquering them and unlocking your full potential on stage.

Physiological manifestations are among the most common and noticeable effects of performance anxiety. As you step onto the stage, you may experience an accelerated heartbeat, an uncontrollable trembling in your fingers, or beads of perspiration forming on your brow. These physical responses, often attributed to the body's natural stress response, can be overwhelming and disrupt your ability to execute your musical passages with precision and control. By acknowledging these physiological signals you can begin to develop strategies to mitigate their impact and regain a sense of calm and composure.

Equally important are the cognitive distortions that arise from performance anxiety. Negative self-talk, self-doubt, and an incessant fear of failure can infiltrate your thoughts and erode your confidence from within. These distortions can cloud your focus, undermine your technical abilities, and create a barrier between you and your musical expression. Recognizing these cognitive patterns is the first step towards dismantling their influence. Through deliberate and mindful practice, you can reframe your thoughts, cultivate self-compassion, and nurture a positive mindset that empowers you to conquer the challenges of performance anxiety.

By shining a light on the effects of performance anxiety, we equip ourselves with the knowledge and awareness necessary to manage and overcome its grip. In the chapters that follow, we will explore a multitude of techniques and strategies that aim to counteract these effects, enabling you to reclaim control of your performance and unlock the true potential that lies within. Remember, you are not alone in this journey, and through dedicated practice and a steadfast commitment to self-improvement, you can transcend the limitations of performance anxiety and embrace the joy and fulfillment that music has to offer.

Unlocking the Power of Imagery

Within the realm of musical performance, the mind holds immense potential to shape our experiences on stage. Visualization, a technique embraced by renowned musicians throughout history, empowers us to harness the power of our imagination and create a mental landscape where success becomes an attainable reality. In this section, we embark on a journey of exploration into the depths of visualization techniques that can transform our mental and emotional preparation for performances.

Visualization is more than a mere daydream; it is a deliberate practice that allows us to mentally rehearse and create vivid images of our desired performance outcomes. By engaging our senses, emotions, and intellect we step into a realm where the boundaries between imagination and reality blur allowing us to transcend the limitations of the physical world. Through consistent and intentional visualization exercises, we unlock a reservoir of confidence, focus, and readiness that elevate our performances to new heights.

To embark on this transformative journey, find a quiet space where you can be fully present with your thoughts. Close your eyes, take a deep breath, and allow yourself to become immersed in the sounds, sights, and sensations of your musical world. Begin by envisioning yourself on the stage, surrounded by the aura of anticipation and excitement. Feel the weight of your instrument in your hands, the texture of the keys or the slide beneath your fingers. Picture the audience before you, their eager faces illuminated by the soft glow of the stage lights. Immerse yourself in the music that flows through you, each note resonating with clarity and intention.

As we navigate this vivid mental landscape, pay attention to the intricate details. Visualize our posture, embodying the poise and grace that emanates from within. Hear the sound of our instrument as it blends harmoniously with the ensemble or fills the concert hall with its rich and captivating tones. Notice the expressions of delight and awe on the faces of the audience as they become enraptured by our performance. Embrace the surge of confidence and assurance that courses through our veins, fueling our every movement and musical expression.

Engaging in regular visualization exercises strengthens our mental fortitude and enhances our ability to perform under pressure. By repeatedly immersing ourselves in this realm of visualization, we are not only shaping our mindset but also programming our subconscious mind to align with our desired outcomes. As we approach the actual performance, the images and sensations we have vividly created in our minds become intertwined with our physical reality, enabling us to step onto the stage with a heightened sense of preparedness and self-assurance.

Remember, visualization is not a substitute for diligent practice, but rather a complementary tool that can amplify the fruits of our efforts. Embrace the power of your imagination, for it has the capacity to shape your reality. By incorporating visualization techniques into our mental and emotional preparation, we embark on a transformative journey that empowers us to shine on stage and share our unique musical voice with the world.

Cultivating Serenity and Focus

In the midst of the whirlwind of anticipation and nerves that often accompany performances, finding a sense of calm and inner peace becomes essential. As musicians, we have the power to tap into the profound connection between our breath, body, and mind to achieve a state of centeredness and focus. In this section, we embark on a journey of exploration into the realm of breathing and relaxation techniques, unveiling the transformative potential they hold in managing performance anxiety and unlocking our true expressive potential.

At the heart of this journey lies the practice of diaphragmatic breathing, a technique embraced by musicians and performers throughout the ages. Unlike shallow chest breathing, diaphragmatic breathing involves the intentional engagement of the diaphragm, a powerful muscle located just below the ribcage. By consciously directing our breath into the depths of our abdomen, we tap into a wellspring of calm and stability.

To experience the transformative power of diaphragmatic breathing, find a comfortable seated position or lie down on your back. Close your eyes and bring your awareness to your breath. Inhale deeply, allowing your belly to expand like a gentle balloon while keeping your chest relatively still. Feel the air filling your lungs, nourishing every cell of your being. As you exhale, let go of any tension or worries, allowing your body to soften and relax.

With each breath, imagine a wave of tranquility washing over you, melting away any knots of tension that may have accumulated within your body. As you cultivate a rhythmic and intentional breathing pattern, feel the profound connection between your breath and your inner state. Notice how your body becomes a vessel for the flow of energy and expression as each inhale invigorates and each exhale releases.

In addition to diaphragmatic breathing, we enter the realm of progressive muscle relaxation, a technique that promotes a deep sense of physical and mental release. Progressive muscle relaxation involves systematically tensing and then releasing different muscle groups, allowing for a profound sense of relaxation and letting go. By consciously bringing attention to our bodies and intentionally releasing the tension, we create the conditions for greater ease and fluidity in our performances.

To practice progressive muscle relaxation, find a comfortable position and bring your awareness to each part of your body starting from your toes and gradually moving upward. As you inhale, tense the muscles in a particular area of your body, such as your feet or hands, and hold the tension for a few seconds. Then, as you exhale, consciously release the tension, allowing the muscles to soften and relax completely. Progressively move through each muscle group, from your feet to your legs, abdomen, chest, arms, and face, experiencing a deep sense of release and relaxation with each breath.

Incorporating these breathing and relaxation techniques into your regular practice routine allows you to cultivate serenity and focus, both in preparation for performances and during the moments of musical expression itself. These practices become invaluable tools in managing performance anxiety as they provide a sanctuary of tranquility amidst the storm of nerves. By consciously connecting with your breath, releasing the tension, and nurturing a state of inner calm, you empower yourself to navigate the stage with grace and confidence.

Remember, the journey of self-discovery and musical growth extends beyond technical proficiency alone. It encompasses the cultivation of a harmonious relationship between body, mind, and spirit. As you embrace the power of breathing and relaxation techniques, you embark on a transformative path toward unlocking your true expressive potential and experiencing the profound joy of music-making.

Harnessing the Power of the Mind

In the realm of musical performance, the mind wields a profound influence on our ability to deliver captivating and confident performances. In this section, we will cover the transformative practices of mental rehearsal and positive affirmations, unlocking the potential of our minds to shape our musical journeys and overcome performance anxiety.

Mental rehearsal, also known as mental practice or mental imagery, is a technique that allows us to mentally rehearse challenging passages and envision successful performances. By vividly imagining ourselves playing with precision and artistry, we create a neural blueprint that paves the way for flawless execution when we step onto the stage. It is a process that goes beyond mere daydreaming; it is an intentional and focused practice that strengthens our musical pathways and enhances our confidence.

To engage in mental rehearsal, find a quiet and comfortable space where you can fully immerse yourself in the practice. Close your eyes and envision the performance scenario with utmost clarity. Visualize yourself holding your instrument, feeling the weight of it in your hands, and sensing the resonance as you play each note. Imagine the stage, the audience, and the ambience of the performance venue. As you mentally navigate challenging passages, feel the precise movements of your fingers, the control of your breath, and the expression emanating from your soul. Embrace the emotions of joy, confidence, and fulfillment that arise from this visualization.

In addition to mental rehearsal, we explore the power of positive affirmations in combating self-doubt and fostering a positive mindset. Positive affirmations are empowering statements that counteract negative self-talk and cultivate self-belief. By consciously choosing and repeating affirmations that resonate with you, you rewire your mind to focus on your strengths, potential, and the limitless possibilities that await you.

Craft affirmations that resonate deeply within you, such as "I am capable of performing with precision and artistry," "My hard work and dedication have prepared me for success," or "I embrace challenges as opportunities for growth." Write these affirmations down and repeat them daily, especially before practice sessions and performances. Let the power of these positive statements seep into your consciousness, replacing doubts and fears with confidence and self-assurance.

By incorporating mental rehearsal and positive self-talk into your practice routine, you cultivate a resilient and empowered performance mindset. These practices not only help you overcome performance anxiety but also deepen your connection with your instrument, your music, and your own artistic voice. Remember, the mind is a powerful ally in your musical journey, and by harnessing its potential you can unlock new realms of artistic expression and perform with unwavering confidence.

Cultivating Comfort and Preparedness

In the realm of musical performance, the moments leading up to taking the stage can be filled with a mix of excitement and nervous anticipation. Pre-performance rituals provide a sanctuary of familiarity and routine, allowing us to cultivate comfort, focus, and a sense of preparedness. In this section, we embark on a journey of discovering and developing personalized pre-performance rituals that enhance our mental and emotional readiness.

Your pre-performance rituals should be tailored to your needs and preferences, encompassing activities that ground you, calm your nerves, and promote a state of focused relaxation. Consider incorporating warm-up exercises specific to your instrument, stretches to release tension from your body, and deep breathing techniques to center your mind. Engage in activities that bring you joy and create a positive mindset, such as listening to inspiring music, reciting affirmations, or engaging in light meditation.

Experiment with different rituals and find a sequence of activities that resonate with you. Consistency is key, as engaging in these rituals repeatedly before performances create a sense of familiarity and security. Remember to allow flexibility within your rituals, adjusting them as needed based on the specific performance context and your evolving needs.

As you establish and embrace your personalized pre-performance rituals, you cultivate a sense of control and preparedness. These rituals become anchors amidst the storm of pre-performance jitters, guiding you into a state of focused readiness. They serve as a bridge between your practice room and the stage, grounding you in the present moment and creating a seamless transition into the world of performance.

Transforming Thoughts for Empowered Performance

Negative thought patterns and self-limiting beliefs can sabotage our performances and contribute to heightened anxiety. In this section, we embark on a transformative exploration of cognitive restructuring techniques, empowering you to identify and challenge negative thoughts and replace them with positive and empowering beliefs. (Rotella, et al. 1995).

The first step in cognitive restructuring is to cultivate self-awareness and recognize the thoughts that arise before, during, and after performances. Notice any patterns of self-doubt, self-criticism, or catastrophic thinking that may arise. These thoughts often stem from a fear of failure, judgment, or not meeting perceived expectations.

Once you have identified these negative thoughts, challenge their validity and replace them with positive and realistic perspectives. Ask yourself, "What evidence do I have to support these negative thoughts? Are there alternative explanations or more balanced viewpoints?" For example, if you catch yourself thinking, "I always make mistakes during performances," challenge this thought by reflecting on past successful performances and acknowledging the growth you have achieved through dedicated practice.

Alongside cognitive restructuring, affirmations play a powerful role in cultivating a positive mindset. Incorporate positive affirmations into your daily practice, both in preparation for performances and during moments of self-reflection. Repeat statements that instill confidence, such as "I am fully prepared to deliver an exceptional performance," "I trust in my abilities to overcome challenges," or "I am deserving of success and recognition." By consistently reinforcing these positive beliefs, you reframe your thoughts and create a mental landscape that nurtures confidence and resilience.

By engaging in cognitive restructuring and embracing positive affirmations, you reshape your mental landscape and transform the way you approach performances. Over time, you build a foundation of self-belief and self-compassion that counteracts performance anxiety and enables you to unleash your full artistic potential.

Embracing the Present Moment

In the realm of performance, the pressure to meet expectations and deliver flawless execution can become overwhelming. However, by embracing acceptance and practicing mindfulness, you can navigate the performance landscape with authenticity, presence, and reduced anxiety.

Acceptance involves acknowledging and embracing the reality of performance anxiety as a natural part of the experience. Recognize that feeling nervous or anxious before a performance does not diminish your abilities or worth as a musician. Allow yourself to release the need for perfection and instead embrace the journey of musical expression with all its imperfections and fluctuations.

Mindfulness, on the other hand, involves cultivating a heightened sense of awareness and non-judgmental observation of the present moment. Before and during performances, bring your attention to the sensations in your body, the sounds surrounding you, and the emotions that arise. Avoid attaching judgments or evaluations to these experiences, allowing them to simply unfold without resistance.

Incorporate mindfulness practices into your daily life to cultivate a state of present-moment awareness. Engage in activities such as meditation, deep breathing exercises, or mindful movement practices like yoga or Tai Chi. As you cultivate mindfulness, you strengthen your ability to focus on the present moment during performances experiencing a heightened connection to your music and a reduced sense of self-consciousness.

Remember, managing performance anxiety is not about eliminating it entirely, but about developing strategies to navigate and channel it effectively. By embracing acceptance and practicing mindfulness, you create a space for authentic expression free from the weight of judgment and fear. Performances become opportunities for genuine connection, self-discovery, and artistic growth.

Through the exploration of pre-performance rituals, cognitive restructuring, and the cultivation of acceptance and mindfulness, you empower yourself to overcome performance anxiety and embrace the fullness of your musical potential. As you integrate these practices into your musical journey, you embark on a path of self-discovery, resilience, and artistic transformation.

CHAPTER 8

Engaging Stage Presence

Having incorporated the techniques and strategies discussed in the preceding chapters, you are now equipped to overcome performance anxiety and deliver mesmerizing and captivating performances. Keep in mind that the stage is not simply a battlefield, but rather a platform for self-expression and connection. Embrace the ongoing journey of mastering your performances, allowing your passion for music to shine through each and every note you play.

As we transition into Chapter 8, our attention turns toward the significance of cultivating an engaging stage presence. It extends beyond technical proficiency, encompassing a variety of elements such as body language, facial expressions, energy projection, and audience interaction.

Stage presence is a powerful form of non-verbal communication that enables you to convey the depth and emotions of the music. It allows you to create an immersive experience that captivates and resonates with your listeners. By refining your stage presence, you enhance your ability to connect with the audience on a profound level, leaving a lasting impact.

Within this chapter, we will explore a range of strategies and techniques for developing an effective stage presence. We will delve into the importance of cultivating body awareness, maintaining a confident posture, and utilizing gestures that convey both musical expression and self-assurance. We will also explore the significance of eye contact, facial expressions, and their ability to convey the essence of the music being performed.

Furthermore, we will discuss methods for fostering a sense of connection with the audience, creating a shared experience that transcends the boundaries of the stage. We will address techniques for managing performance anxiety and harnessing nervous energy to fuel dynamic stage presence. By embracing the stage as a platform for authentic self-expression, we can go beyond technical mastery and truly communicate through our music.

Through the cultivation of engaging stage presence, we not only elevate our own performance experiences, but also forge a profound connection with our listeners. We possess the power to transport them into the world of music, evoke emotions, and create transformative moments of beauty. Our stage presence becomes a conduit through which the music can touch the hearts and souls of those who have the privilege of witnessing our performances.

Join me now as we embark on an exploration of the art of engaging stage presence. Together, we will uncover the transformative impact it can have on our performances, allowing our presence on stage to become a vessel for sharing our unique musical voice. Let us unlock the secrets of stage charisma, foster an authentic connection with the audience, and create performances that linger in the memory long after the final notes have faded.

Are you ready to embark on this exhilarating journey of mastering stage presence? With confidence, grace, and a deep sense of purpose, let us step into the spotlight. The stage awaits us, ready to showcase the transformative power of our music.

Connecting with the Audience

When you step onto the stage, you have the power to create a transformative experience for your audience. Connecting with them on a deep level goes beyond playing the right notes or executing technical passages flawlessly. It involves tapping into the emotional essence of the music and conveying its message with sincerity and authenticity. In this section, we will delve into the art of connecting with your audience.

One powerful technique for connecting with your audience is through musical communication. Music has the ability to transcend language barriers and evoke profound emotions. We will explore how to communicate through your music using techniques such as phrasing, dynamics, and musical interpretation. By understanding the nuances of the music and infusing it with your personal expression, you can create performances that resonate deeply with your listeners.

Engaging with your audience is another crucial aspect of connecting with them. We will discuss techniques for establishing a rapport and building a relationship with your listeners. This includes acknowledging their presence, making eye contact, and inviting them into your musical journey. Create a warm and inviting atmosphere and you can make your audience feel like active participants in the performance rather than passive observers.

Furthermore, we will explore the power of evoking emotional responses from your audience. Music has the ability to stir emotions and create a shared experience between performer and listener. We will delve into techniques for harnessing the emotional depth of the music and delivering performances that touch the hearts of your audience. Understanding the emotional landscape of the music and connecting with its inherent beauty will help you create performances that leave a lasting impact.

Body Language and Posture

Your body language is an essential component of your stage presence. It communicates non-verbally to your audience, conveying confidence, professionalism, and engagement with the music. In this section, we will discuss the impact of body language on stage presence and audience perception.

Adopting confident and open postures is key to commanding attention and projecting a sense of authority on stage. We will explore techniques for standing tall, with your shoulders relaxed, and your body aligned. This conveys a sense of self-assurance and professionalism to your audience. Additionally, we will delve into the importance of facial expressions in conveying the emotional depth of your music. Your face is a powerful tool for expressing the nuances and subtleties of the music. We will explore techniques for maintaining a calm and focused expression, while also allowing your emotions to shine through.

Gestures and movements also play a significant role in enhancing your stage presence. We will discuss techniques for using your hands and arms to express the shape and dynamics of the music. By incorporating purposeful gestures that align with the musical phrases, you can visually enhance the audience's understanding and appreciation of the music. We will also explore the importance of eye contact in establishing a connection with your audience. Making eye contact with individuals in the audience creates a sense of intimacy and invites them into your musical world.

By consciously using body language to support your musical expression, you enhance your stage presence and captivate your audience. When your body language aligns with the emotions and intentions of the music, it becomes a powerful vehicle for conveying your artistic vision.

Managing Performance Mistakes

In the realm of live performance, mistakes are inevitable. They can be a source of anxiety and self-doubt, but they also present an opportunity for growth and resilience. In this section, we will provide strategies for gracefully managing performance mistakes.

Maintaining composure in the face of unexpected challenges is crucial. We will explore techniques for staying calm and focused, even when mistakes occur. This includes learning to let go of perfectionism and embracing imperfections as part of the artistic process. By maintaining a sense of poise and professionalism, you can navigate through mistakes without allowing them to derail your performance.

Adapting at the moment is another essential skill in managing performance mistakes. We will discuss strategies for making quick adjustments and improvisations when things don't go as planned. This includes developing a strong internal musical compass that guides you through unforeseen circumstances. By cultivating your listening skills and being attuned to the music in the present moment, you can make intuitive decisions that keep the performance flowing seamlessly.

Redirecting your focus back to the music is crucial when mistakes occur. We will explore techniques for shifting your attention away from the mistake and towards the overall musical experience. By maintaining a strong connection to the music and staying committed to its expressive qualities, you can minimize the impact of mistakes and deliver a captivating performance.

Embracing a resilient mindset and staying grounded in the present moment will help you navigate performance mistakes with confidence and grace. Remember that mistakes are not indicative of your worth as a musician, but rather opportunities for growth and learning. With a focused and resilient mindset, you can transform mistakes into moments of artistic expression and connection with your audience.

Incorporating the strategies and techniques outlined in this chapter equip you to conquer performance anxiety and deliver compelling and engaging performances. Remember, the stage is not merely a battleground but a platform for self-expression and connection. Embrace the journey of performance mastery and let your passion for music shine through every note you play.

CHAPTER 9

Collaborative Practice with Other Trombonists

Now, as we delve into Chapter 9, we shift our focus toward the power of collaborative practice with other trombonists. While individual practice forms the foundation of our musical development, engaging in collaborative experiences with fellow trombonists takes our playing to new heights. Through collaboration, we tap into the collective energy and creativity of a group, sparking inspiration and mutual growth.

Collaborative practice offers a wealth of benefits for trombonists. It cultivates ensemble skills, fosters a deep sense of musical communication, and provides an opportunity for shared learning. Together, we can explore different interpretations, refine our ensemble blend and balance, and strive for unified musical expression.

In this chapter, we will explore various ways to engage in collaborative practice with other trombonists. We will delve into ensemble playing, chamber music, trombone choirs, and other group settings that allow us to connect and create music together. We will discuss the importance of active listening, effective communication, and developing a strong sense of rhythmic and tonal cohesion.

Through collaborative practice we not only enhance our technical and musical skills, but we also develop invaluable qualities such as teamwork, adaptability, and responsiveness. By working with other trombonists, we learn to navigate the intricacies of ensemble dynamics, to blend our individual voices into a cohesive whole, and to collectively bring a musical composition to life.

So, join me as we explore the art of collaborative practice with other trombonists. Let us discover the joy of making music together, the exhilaration of shared artistic expression, and the transformative power of musical collaboration. Together, we will unlock new dimensions of our playing, forge lasting musical connections, and create unforgettable musical experiences.

Are you ready to embark on this exciting journey of collaborative practice? Let us begin, and let our trombones resonate in harmony as we explore the limitless possibilities that await us in the realm of collective music-making.

Collaboration is Wondrous

Collaborating and practicing with fellow trombonists is an invaluable experience for musicians. We should actively seek opportunities to learn from and engage with our fellow trombonists. Participating in trombone ensembles or chamber groups provides a unique chance to explore the distinctive sound and musical expression that is specific to the trombone.

Through collaborative practice with other trombonists, we can gain insights into different playing techniques, tone production methods, and musical interpretations. I encourage you to attentively listen and observe your peers, paying close attention to the nuances and approaches that contribute to a distinctive trombone sound.

Attending masterclasses or workshops that are tailored to trombone playing is another way for us to engage in collaborative learning. These events create a platform for trombonists to come together, exchange knowledge, and learn from experienced trombone players and teachers. We should actively participate in these sessions, asking questions, and embracing the opportunity to collaborate and connect with other trombonists.

Collaborative practice cultivates a sense of camaraderie and shared learning among trombonists. Engage in musical conversations with your fellow trombonists, discussing different sound concepts, techniques, and repertoire. By exchanging ideas and experiences, we can broaden our understanding of trombone sounds and develop our own unique approach.

Organizing trombone section rehearsals or trombone quartets provides a close-knit collaborative setting where you can work closely with your peers. In this environment, you can focus on blending your sounds, refining intonation, and cultivating a cohesive ensemble sound specific to the trombone section. Highlight the importance of active listening and effective communication within the group to achieve a unified and balanced sound.

Embracing collaborative practice with other trombonists allows us to enhance our understanding of trombone sound and technique while developing important skills such as ensemble playing, teamwork, and adaptability. Collaboration among trombonists creates a supportive and inspiring environment where we can learn from one another, grow as musicians, and cultivate their own distinct trombone sounds

Collaborative practice is an essential aspect of trombone playing, allowing students to learn from and collaborate with their peers to enhance their musical abilities. To foster this collaborative spirit, an assignment can be designed to encourage trombonists to engage in various activities that promote teamwork and shared learning. These assignments provide opportunities for students to work together in ensembles, analyze and discuss different interpretations, and explore new musical ideas. By participating in these collaborative assignments, students not only improve their trombone skills but also develop crucial communication, listening, and ensemble playing abilities. These assignments create a supportive environment where trombonists can inspire and challenge one another, fostering a deeper understanding of their instrument and the joy of making music together.

Fostering Musical Connections: Collaborative Practice Assignments

- Trombone Ensemble Arrangement: Assign students to form trombone ensembles of varying sizes (duets, trios, quartets, etc.) and task them with arranging a piece of music specifically for trombone ensemble. They can collaborate on selecting suitable repertoire, dividing parts, and rehearsing together to achieve a cohesive ensemble sound.

- Virtual Collaboration Project: In the age of technology, students can engage in virtual collaboration projects where they record their individual trombone parts and combine them into a virtual ensemble performance. Assign a piece of music or allow students to choose their own, and guide them on recording techniques, synchronization, and audio mixing. Encourage them to communicate and provide feedback to one another throughout the process.

- Trombone Section Rehearsal Observation: Pair students up and have them observe each other's trombone section rehearsals. Each student takes turns attending the other's section rehearsal and provides constructive feedback on section blend, balance, intonation, and overall sound. This assignment promotes active listening, critical evaluation, and collaborative learning within the trombone section.

- Collaborative Interpretation Analysis: Assign students to form small groups and select a specific piece of trombone repertoire. Each group analyzes different interpretations of the same piece by renowned trombonists. They collaborate to compare and contrast the various approaches, discussing sound production, articulation, phrasing, and expressive nuances. Students can then apply what they have learned to their own performances.

- Trombone Masterclass Workshop: Organize a trombone masterclass workshop where students take turns performing solo repertoire in front of their peers. Encourage active participation and feedback from both the performers and the audience. Students can collaborate by offering suggestions, sharing performance tips, and discussing sound production techniques, resulting in a collective learning experience.

- Trombone Quartet Composition: Challenge students to form trombone quartets and compose original music specifically for this ensemble. They can collaborate on creating unique compositions, and exploring different musical styles and techniques. Encourage them to experiment with harmonies, textures, and rhythmic variations, fostering creativity and collaboration within the quartet.

- Collaborative Warm-up Routine: Assign students to collaborate on creating a warm-up routine specifically for trombone players. Each student can contribute different exercises or techniques they find beneficial. They can then combine their individual contributions to create a comprehensive warm-up routine that covers various aspects of sound production, flexibility, articulation, and technique. The collaborative warm-up routine can be shared and used by all students for their daily practice sessions.

These assignments encourage students to actively engage in collaborative practice, learn from one another, and develop essential skills in ensemble playing, communication, and musical interpretation. Collaborative practice not only strengthens their trombone skills but also fosters a sense of community and shared learning among trombonists.

AFTERWORD

The Journey Continues

As we reach the conclusion of this book, we find ourselves at the threshold of a new chapter in our musical journey. Throughout the preceding chapters, we have explored the fundamental aspects of trombone playing, delved into techniques for sound development, and discussed the importance of cultivating a unique musical voice. We have also examined the role of practice routines, explored the benefits of collaborative learning, and emphasized the significance of active listening. Now, armed with these insights and knowledge, we are ready to embark on a lifelong pursuit of musical excellence.

The adventure of a musician is one that never truly ends. It is a continuous path of growth, exploration, and self-discovery. As trombonists, we have the privilege of being part of a rich and diverse musical tradition. Our instrument has a long history that spans across genres and cultures, and it is our responsibility to honor and contribute to this legacy.

In the pursuit of excellence, we must remember that progress is not always linear. There will be moments of triumph and moments of frustration, but each experience is an opportunity for growth. It is important to embrace challenges and setbacks as learning opportunities, for it is through these obstacles that we develop resilience and fortitude.

Collaboration lies at the heart of our musical journey. Whether it is playing in ensembles, attending masterclasses, or engaging in musical conversations with peers, the power of collaboration cannot be overstated. Through working alongside other musicians, we broaden our understanding of sound, develop our ensemble skills, and cultivate a sense of community and shared learning. Collaborative practice assignments can serve as valuable tools to enhance our musical development and foster meaningful connections with fellow trombonists.

Sound aesthetics play a pivotal role in our musical expression. By exploring different musical contexts and genres, we expand our sonic palette and find our unique musical identity. Drawing inspiration from renowned musicians known for their distinctive sound, we can analyze and emulate aspects of their playing while still maintaining our individuality. Integrating sound development exercises into our repertoire practice allows us to enhance our musical interpretation, adapt to different styles, and continually refine our sound.

Active listening serves as a gateway to musical growth. By immersing ourselves in a wide range of recordings and performances, we develop a discerning ear and expand our musical horizons. Through focused listening, we can analyze and appreciate the nuances of sound production, tone quality, and musical expression. This deepened understanding of sound translates into more meaningful and informed musical performances.

As we conclude this book, let us remember that our musical journey is not confined to these pages. It is a lifelong commitment to continuous learning, growth, and self-improvement. Let us approach each practice session with curiosity, dedication, and a passion for our craft. Let us seek opportunities to collaborate, to share our knowledge, and to learn from others. And above all, let us never lose sight of the joy and fulfillment that music brings to our lives.

May the knowledge and insights gained from this book serve as a guide and inspiration as you continue your journey as a trombonist. Remember, the journey is as important as the destination, and every step you take brings you closer to becoming the musician you aspire to be. Keep playing, keep learning, and keep embracing the beautiful and transformative power of music. The adventure awaits.

ACKNOWLEDGEMENTS

I would like to express my gratitude to those who have contributed to the creation of this book. My teachers and mentors, not exclusively trombonists, but educators who have gone above and beyond to make sure their students excel for generations to come both in Venezuela and in the United States. My colleagues and peers whose influence have heavily shaped many of the ideas I have developed to produce a concise teaching philosophy that interrelates both performance and pedagogy as two sides of the same coin. The institutions that have given me the opportunity to impart knowledge and ideas, but especially have given me the honor to learn from their students teaching me the importance of the realization that our students are always our best teachers. The universities that saw in me the potential to become part of their student bodies and gave me the opportunity to come to this beautiful country, embracing me as one of their own. My team of collaborators, peer-mentors, and colleagues led by Dr. Jose Valentino Ruiz whose expertise continues to amaze me and who has taught me how to discover my own potential. Last but not least, my former and current students, who are living proof of the results of everything that this book contains. Your successes are the ultimate achievement of this practical and theoretical method because it speaks my heart through all of you.

Thank you.

BIBLIOGRAPHY

Clear, J. (2018). *Atomic Habits*. Avery at Penguin Random House LLC.

Frederiksen, B. (1996). *Arnold Jacobs: Song and Wind*. Windsong Press Limited.

Green, B., & Gallwey, T. (1986). *The Inner Game of Music*. Doubleday

Rotella, B. (1995). *Golf Is Not a Game of Perfect*. Simon & Schuster.

Ruiz, J.V. (2016). *The Effects of Technical and Imagery-based Instruction on Aspiring Performing Artists' Acquisition of Learning Newly Composed Pieces and Improvisation and on Listeners' Perceived Expressivity*. Ph.D. Dissertation University of South Florida.

BIOGRAPHIES

About the Author

Dr. José Leonardo Leon is a renowned musician with expertise in classical, commercial, and global music styles. Leon is a sought-after trombonist for orchestral, chamber, and solo performances, as well as studio recordings for various genres, and he has been featured in music videos with multi-million media impressions/streams. Dr. Leon is currently the Visiting Professor of Music (Applied Trombone) and Founder and Coordinator of the Initiative for Arts Performance and Entrepreneurship at Florida Atlantic University's College of Arts and Letters. A Bach Brass and Conn-Selmer Artist, Leon expresses his performative and entrepreneurial career as a trombonist for several orchestras in Florida and also serves as an Editorial Board Member for the International Journal of Music Entrepreneurship & Leadership. In 2023, Leon became the recipient of the International Academy of

Digital Arts and Sciences 2023 Anthem Award for Education, Arts, and Culture—Strategy. Moreover, Leon served as Bass Trombonist for the 2015 Latin Grammy Award-winning Best Instrumental Album and has won three Global Music Awards in the categories of Contemporary Classical Albums (twice), Producer, and Composition. For more information, please visit www.joseleonardoleon.com.

About the Foreword Author

Dr. José Valentino Ruiz is a world-renowned arts entrepreneur, multi-instrumentalist, composer, producer, and professor. A four-time GRAMMY® Award Winner, EMMY® Award Winner, and 15-time Global Music® Award Winner, is maintaining a vibrant career as an internationally touring cross-genre performing and recording artist (flutist, saxophonist, and bassist). With over 1400 concerts as a headlining artist on six continents, he has graced festivals, performing arts centers, and conferences. Ruiz has also led 40+ non-profit mission trips, delivered 110+ keynotes, concerts, and workshops in academic sectors, consulted numerous Fortune 500 companies, produced 140+ albums and 10 documentaries, and published 54 peer-reviewed research articles. He currently holds the positions of Resident Media Composer at Hayden5, CEO at JV Music Enterprises, Founding Program Coordinator of UF Music Business & Entrepreneurship, Director of the Global Institute for Music Research's Commission for Entrepreneurship and Leadership, and Co-Editor of *Artivate: A Journal of Entrepreneurship in the Arts*.

www.ingramcontent.com/pod-product-compliance
Lightning Source LLC
Chambersburg PA
CBHW042129100526
44587CB00026B/4229